Reflections on my First Year as Principal

Collected by Robert J. Kealey, Ed. D.

NATIONAL CATHOLIC EDUCATIONAL ASSOCIATION

ISBN #1-55833-257X

Table of Contents

Preface

This book grew out of the first principals' academies for beginning principals that NCEA held in February 2000. Almost 60 principals, all in their first or second year as principals of Catholic elementary/middle schools, from all over the United States attended this program. During their five days together, they became immersed in the theme of the academy, "Enhancing the Identity of the Catholic School." These principals heard several speakers discuss this topic; they had time to reflect on it, and they shared ideas with one another.

At the conclusion of the academy, the principals were asked to write a brief essay relating their most memorable experience of their first year as principal. This was the price that the principals had to pay for attending the academy, which had the corporate support of CTB/McGraw-Hill. NCEA wanted to publish these essays and use the publication as a means of encouraging teachers to consider assuming the role of educational leader, principal. This book will certainly serve this purpose. However, we believe that all educational leaders should read this work reflectively. Diocesan school office personnel will gain new insights into what beginning principals need. Professors of courses to train administrators will discover what needs to be changed in their programs for training future principals. Beginning principals will be affirmed in their role. Experienced principals will become re-energized in their ministry of Catholic education. Teachers will learn of the joys of this leadership role. Priests will learn again how the Catholic school is a ministry of the Catholic Church and an important part of the evangelizing mission of the parish. Parents will be comforted by the fact that their children are in the hands of confident and truly spiritual people.

Each of the essays tells the story of one individual. While each of the stories is different and reflects the individual style of the person, they all share a common theme. Catholic school principals hold deep spiritual beliefs and manifest great dedication to helping children. The writers were not writing to impress the reader, but the reflective reader must be impressed with these stories.

The NCEA Department of Elementary Schools expresses its gratitude to the principals who shared their very personal thoughts with the entire Catholic community. Michelle Rimar edited the essays, developed the chapter titles, and placed the essays into these chapters. The association is grateful to her for her thoughtful work. Beatriz Ruiz of the NCEA Computer Graphics Department designed the cover and laid out the book.

The department offers this book to the members of the association with the hope that it will inspire all of us to rededicate ourselves to the ministry of Catholic education.

Robert J. Kealey, Ed.D.
Executive Director

James Brennan, Ed.D.
President

Department of Elementary Schools
National Catholic Educational Association
Feast of the Presentation 2001

Chapter 1: Making Changes and Building From the Ground Up

Connections: Building a Stronger Community

Sharon Bresler
St. Thomas School
Fort Thomas, Kentucky

Being a principal of a Catholic school was not really on my agenda for the 1999-2000 school year. But, as we all know, God works in mysterious ways, and sometimes all we can do is hold on and pray as He works His wonders through our lives. When I thought of all the responsibilities I would be facing as an administrator (head catechist, instructional leader, safety coordinator, and school nurse to name a few), I didn't realize that my most important and rewarding role would be part mediator and part publicity agent.

When I first took over leadership of Saint Thomas School, I sent out questionnaires to the people in leadership positions (The board of total Catholic education, the parish council, the two parent groups who support the school, etc.), and to the faculty I inherited. I explained in the accompanying letter that I was trying to get the pulse of the parish, to find out what was important to the leaders of the parish and the school. Before I could make any suggestions or changes I needed to know and understand the parish and people with whom I would be working.

The replies stated clearly that the main reason for the school was the continuity of the Catholic faith: the spirituality of our religion should be the main focus of the school, with high academic standards a very close second. Another focus that was emphasized was the need to rebuild the community between the school and the parish due to a rather lengthy feud between their prior leadership. It was then that I had the first inkling as to why God may have sent me to St. Thomas School. I have always been told that I am a good listener and communicator with the ability to see both sides of any situation. These strengths have made this first year a lot more manageable.

At our first in-service, before school started, my faculty and I brainstormed ideas for our school theme, knowing that this would set the course for the entire school year. We settled on the theme, "God Connects Us All." My faculty devised several ideas and programs to help bridge the gap between the school, the parish, the community, and the world. This was a rather ambitious goal; however, my faculty was convinced that with the proper push and the right public relations we could accomplish plenty.

We started small and with the people we had the most influence over – our students!

In order to bring the children within the school closer together, we began a Big Brother/Big Sister program. Our sixth, seventh, and eighth graders were paired with our kindergarten, first, and second graders respectively. We did this in an effort to instill leadership and responsibility in our older children and at the same time help the youngest in our school to feel a part of the community. As the students progress through the grades, they will keep their same partners, culminating with the second and eighth graders sharing the sacramental years.

Once the school felt like home to students we decided to widen our reach, and involve the parish!

We began to involve the PREP (Parish Religious Education Program) as pen pals and prayer partners. We started retreats for all of the sacramental preparation classes so the school children and the PREP children could meet before the sacrament. This definitely had a unifying effect that we will continue to nurture.

Although we did many things throughout the year to bring the parish and school together, I think the program that has had the most remarkable success has been our technology committee. I saw improved technology an area of extreme importance to the school. A committee was formed to study the problem and to come up with solutions within our limited budget. This committee comprised of administration, staff, and parish members who had expertise in this area. The unified committee decided that the first order of business was to rewire the computer lab, get computers in all the classrooms, and network both school buildings. We needed leadership, knowledge, funding, and manpower to accomplish these goals. We had planning meetings, then at intervals parent and community volunteers came up to school to drill holes, run wire, and network all the computers. Word began to spread as a result of so much time and energy going into our technology department, and one parishioner got his company to make a matching donation of $2,500 earmarked specifically for technology.

We currently have internal e-mail and are getting the entire faculty comfortable with their classroom computers via several in-services, before bringing in the Internet next fall. As a sign of ongoing support, the two parent organizations have each agreed to purchase up to six computers per year. We have also applied for the E-Rate sponsored by the Federal Communication Commission, as well as several grants to help defray the enormous cost of the constant upkeep of technology. Our technology committee will continue to guide us with further decision making.

Soon we began involving the whole community in our school projects!

As the year progressed, some community businesses began to upgrade their computers and they donated the older models to us. Besides restocking our computer lab, we were able to put a computer in every classroom. Keeping with our push for technology, and trying to make the community more aware of what we have to offer, our technology coordinator and our eighth-grade tech team, developed a school Web page. The address is http://www.members.home.net/sttschool.

We also consulted a community florist about a greenhouse we received from a grant. They agreed to come and speak with classes about proper use of a greenhouse once ours is set up.

We then broadened our wings to touch the whole world!

Closing the gap between the school, parish, and community wasn't enough. I wanted our students to become a part of the worldwide community and experience the feeling of helping others. Through discussion, the teachers decided to adopt a nearby Appalachian mission. Throughout the year, grade levels were assigned different months and asked to raise money for our mission. Most grades chose to have a bake sale, but we also had some raffles and a "blue jeans for bucks" (out of uniform) day. Overall, we've raised approximately $500.00. We also collected personal cleansing products.

Looking back on this year, I find that not only did I encourage our students and staff to bridge the gap and establish a new framework for upcoming years, but also I saw myself stretch my abilities and move beyond my personal expectations. This has been a challenging year in the areas of publicity, discipline, faculty in-services, and many unexpected occurrences, yet I have continued to put my trust in God and believe that I'm here for a reason. No matter what I'm facing, all things are made easier with prayer.

Building New Friendships while Changing Old Ways

Raymond F. Karlin
Saint Hyacinth Academy
San Jacinto, California

Upon entering a principalship, one begins to hear the stories of pastors who are difficult to work with, long time secretaries who undermine your authority, experienced teachers who will fight the new system, and parents who will challenge your patience to the point of complete exhaustion. Do these events happen? I'm sure they do. Add a few unruly students to the mix and one has to think, "What am I getting myself into?" Luckily, my experience may be the exception to the rule. I could not have had a better year!

I pray that every principal in his or her first year have the opportunity to work for a pastor who is as caring and open as Fr. Gerry Leonard. Without hesitation, he took a chance on hiring someone with no previous principal experience for a job that clearly needed an experienced hand. Then, he demonstrated the faith he had in me by allowing me to do my job by offering support when I requested it. It's vitally important that the principal and pastor work together and have a clear understanding of their roles. I could not have asked for a better partner in my first year.

A good secretary is the lifeblood of any organization. I don't know what I would have done without Mrs. Ter Best. She was my right and left arm. No amount of words could reflect the appreciation I have for her efforts throughout the year.

Change is always difficult, no matter how open one is to it. My first desire was to change very little and spend the first year observing to develop a plan of action the following year. Soon after arriving, I decided that some changes needed to be made immediately to set the tone for changes to come. Did I have a few problems with teachers and parents? Yes, I did. But by and large, they demonstrated an enthusiasm that was clearly Spirit-driven to do what was needed to further the school. I found it a privilege to work with such a fine group of people.

I spent some time trying to isolate an experience that I would consider being my most rewarding experience of the year; I could not. I felt the whole year was rewarding. I learned a great deal. I met many new friends. I feel that I grew in my own faith after experiencing the Spirit that was present at the school. After fifteen years in education, I was re-energized. My most rewarding experience this year was the opportunity to grow both professionally and spiritually with the help of a fine supporting cast.

Through Hard Work and Faith, a School is Reborn

Karen Fox
St. Charles School
Coldwater, Michigan

When I accepted the position as principal of St. Charles School in 1998, I accepted a gigantic challenge. The school had been closed since 1968 because of a fire, and all records and past programs were gone. There was no pattern to follow. It was a new beginning, not only for myself, but for the school and staff members as well. When the school reopened in 1998, I was a first-year principal with 6 first-year teachers, a first-year secretary, and a pastor who had never had a school before. We were all novices!

Goals had been set by the feasibility committee, which studied and planned the school's reopening. Since there were no educators on this committee, there was little understanding of the steps necessary to accomplish these goals, and no program was left out. I found myself grappling with state licensing for a preschool program as well as a before and after school day care program. I had to research the laws to secure transportation and special classes through the public school system. Fortunately, the gentleman who had spearheaded the feasibility study was also a lawyer and very helpful in this aspect.

My first days on the job found me in a school building originally built in 1911, which was being renovated, painted and brought up to code. There were no phones, no computers, and no working bathrooms. I spent the months of June and July getting the curriculum set, ordering books, and assisting parent volunteers, who were renovating the school. Parents were involved in many aspects of the school's reopening. They were putting in a playground, planting a Mary Garden, which runs along the side of the school, ordering products that they felt were needed, and generally trying to be of assistance. Their enthusiasm was catching, and many became involved. Furniture, file cabinets, classroom supplies, etc. were arriving daily and being stacked in the basement. Throughout the summer, we worked diligently to prepare for the year ahead.

The school reopened on September 1, 1998. The student body consisted of 85 students in preschool through fifth grade. Most of these students had attended one of the six elementary schools in the district. It was a challenge to implement a curriculum that would meet their diverse needs. Because of the small numbers, some classes were combined. Students received more individualized attention and we became one large family.

Our Catholic identity is the very heart of the school. The first thing you see as you enter the school is Jesus holding a "welcome" sign. This immediately identifies Him as the reason for our school. We plan weekly children's masses, join together for frequent recitation of the rosary, familiarize students with the saints, share daily prayer and petitions, and teach specific lessons on our faith.

In order to do service for others, each class has a service project. Their charitable activities include visiting the nursing homes, helping Meals on Wheels, bringing food for the hungry, making cards and praying for the sick, earning money through a math-a-thon for St. Jude's Hospital, sacrificing for the Holy Childhood Association, and making birthday bags for poor children.

We are building community between the families of St. Charles Parish by having activities that include school families as well as families who do not have children in the school. In the fall we have a Harvest Dinner and Basket Raffle, which is a pot luck dinner with drinks and desserts furnished by the school. Baskets filled by the school children are raffled. In March, we have a Mardi Gras Auction. Admittance and food are free. School families, Knights of Columbus, Church guilds, and parishioners work cooperatively to make this a gala, enjoyable event. Both activities provide an opportunity for socialization and community building.

By the fall of 1999 our numbers had grown to 125. Many skeptics, who held back to see how things went the first year, joined our ranks. We had proven that we were a stable school with a strong curriculum, excellent teachers, and daily spiritual experiences. We had managed to get through the first year! Parental involvement, staff input, pastor support, and cooperation of the parishioners were instrumental in the revival of St. Charles School. Another strong support group is the past alumni of St. Charles School. They have a true sense of pride in seeing the school they graduated from being reborn.

Another feasibility study was conducted this year to discern if a sixth grade should be added in the 2000-2001 school year. This plan calls for a seventh grade in 2001-2002 and an eighth grade in 2002-2003. It was decided that the student population and finances were available to pursue this goal. Recently, land was donated to the parish to build a new elementary and middle school. This will be another exciting challenge.

I have joined various committees and educational groups of the public school system and intermediate school district in order for our students to be included in public school-funded enrichment activities whenever possible. I am involved in all committees of the school board as it strives to set the pace for the school's future years. I attend the Religious Education Commission Meetings to collaborate with the CCD teachers.

Although the past two years have been extremely challenging and exhausting, they have also been very rewarding. Reopening a school as a novice with a novice staff was a leap of faith. I am proud to have taken that leap and feel a true sense of accomplishment. With the Lord's help, I have been instrumental in leading the staff, students and parents. Together we have set the tone for the school. The foundation has been laid for future growth with the school's mission statement:

> "St. Charles School is a Catholic school whose mission is to provide each child with a firm foundation of Catholic values, academic knowledge and life experiences. We are dedicated to the education of the entire child: spiritually, academically, socially, and emotionally. St. Charles School shares in a partnership with parents to nurture our children, promote worship through prayer and liturgy, communicate the gospel message to students, stress the importance of service to others, and provide opportunities to build community."

Sowing the Seeds of New School Spirit

Susan K. Perry
St. Clement of Rome
Metairie, Louisiana

I became a principal after spending my entire career in Catholic education at the elementary/middle school level. My experiences and education as a teacher of English, math, social studies, and gifted studies as well as a brief stint as a librarian have afforded me a unique and comprehensive view of the workings and needs of a Catholic elementary school. Often in professional meetings of principals, the question is asked, "How many of you thought one day you would be sitting here as a principal?" I can honestly say that that thought never once crossed my mind. I was very happy with the daily interaction with children of various ages and in various capacities. So, you might say that I was chosen for this job. The hand that tapped me was the hand of my former principal who said he recognized leadership and administrative talents in me. I prayed that the hand of God was involved in this decision, and after my few short months as principal, I am convinced it was.

In pondering the question of what has been my most

memorable experience as a new principal, I realize that there has not been one single experience but a series of related experiences that have made my year rewarding. These experiences are all related to the fact that I am finally able to put into effect many ideas and much knowledge that I have accumulated over the years in my various capacities in Catholic education. I was able to see a book-writing project that I initiated as a seventh grade English teacher to be taken to new levels under the direction of an enthusiastic teacher. I was able to advise and encourage first-grade teachers who were setting up centers in their classrooms for the first time. I was able to give the thumbs up for a highly successful family math night. I was able to lead the teachers in "dancing" at our parish fair, an event with no precedent and one which parents and parishioners alike are still extolling. I was able to laugh with the teacher who was voted to kiss a pig at the fair, a fund-raising event of unparalleled success.

This has been a successful year so far, but not one without the usual trials and tribulations inherent with such a responsible and rather formidable position. Not every parent or teacher has been happy with my every decision, but every one has had the opportunity to voice his or her opinion with me in a calm and collaborative manner. My open-door policy has enabled students, parents, and staff to stop by for any reason, and that fact has truly given me the reputation of being approachable.

If I had to focus on what specifically has made this year rewarding, I would have to say that seeing academic and curriculum ideas I initiated come to fruition is the most personally satisfying. For years, parents and teachers have asked for the inclusion of a foreign language program. Next year, all students will have Spanish in their schedule. Students wanted additional electives, and next year various exploratory courses will be offered to middle school students. Students wanted more fun activities, and this year pep rallies, dress down days, and field trips enhanced the school day. Parents expressed concern about the volume of homework students have, especially at the middle-school level. Next year, all middle school students will have a supervised study hall once a week to help alleviate the homework burden. Teachers came to me as one not very far removed from the classroom. Their requests have often been met with affirmatives, or at least the reasons for denial have been explained and reasonably discussed. This is a very pleasant working environment, and the teacher retention rate is extremely high.

Three specific incidents can sum up the fulfilling nature of my first year as principal of St. Clement of Rome School. At one faculty meeting, I very soberly said that I had an important announcement to make. The content of that announcement is not important, but the effect on one teacher was. She came to me after the meeting and said that her heart sank because she thought I was announcing my resignation. How relieved she was to know that I was definitely going to be around for awhile. Another affirmation occurred after our very enjoyable and highly successful Mardi Gras Math Night. One parent came up to me, thanking me for the evening. After I gave full credit to the teachers involved, the parent patted me on the back and said, "I love this new administration!" And finally, I recently had a conversation with another principal who taught at my school many years ago, long before my time. He said he had heard good things about me and that I reminded him of Sr. Consillio, a lovely Irish Presentation Sister whose order founded St. Clement School. I could not have been more complimented than to be compared to one who embodied the true Catholic presence in our school. Every day I thank God for the opportunity to serve Him through the students of St. Clement of Rome School, and I humbly ask for His help to maintain that Catholic environment and spirit upon which this school was established.

Creating an Oasis of Stability in Turbulent Times

Kim McGeorge
Our Lady of Good Counsel
Little Rock, Arkansas

The most rewarding experience of my first few months here at Our Lady of Good Counsel School is simply establishing stability in the school. I am the third principal this school year, and the sixth in the last five years!

When I first came in November, parents kept telling me they heard rumors that I was leaving! It has taken some time to alleviate their fears, but hopefully they understand that I am here for the long run. The students thought this too, and it was very difficult, at first, for them to understand that I was here to stay.

Many rules and regulations that were established, but not enforced, were reestablished to provide much needed order in the school. Not all my efforts towards this end have been appreciated, although I think everyone can see the difference in how the school is being run and the necessity of having order to enhance the learning environment.

I have a vision of where I see Our Lady of Good Counsel going and the type of school I see us becoming. We are steeped in many wonderful traditions that I would never dream of changing, but we also have a very bright future, filled with new ideas, technology, and experiences that could only enhance our present traditions. The many cultures represented by our students, parents, and faculty foster a spirit of understanding and acceptance toward all people. This Christ-like spirit is one of the many blessings I've received since I've come here.

I love being the principal of Our Lady of Good Counsel, and I love the possibilities that being here, during this time in our history, can entail. Like the song says, "Our future's so bright, we gotta wear shades!"

Chapter 2:
Creating Beauty From the Inside Out

A Community of Faith

Donna Woodard
St. Patrick
Belle Plaine, Minnesota

Edwin Markham once said "No one goes his way alone; all that we send into the lives of others comes back into our own." Those words seem to strike a key with those of us who serve in the ministry of Catholic education. Whether we minister as a teacher or administrator, in a new school or old, we all serve God by ministering to His children.

Throughout my first year as principal I was faced with what I now know are the "usual" obstacles. However, at the time I felt that I was always holding an umbrella waiting for the next storm. The community of St. Patrick taught me a great deal about God's plan and call for us all to work together. We are all the body of Christ. We can accomplish so much more when we work a common mission, to spread the Good News among God's people. The mission of our Catholic schools is to teach children that their faith and its journey is lifelong, and should be a part of who we are at all times.

The teachers and staff showed me that no matter how young or old we are, we can always learn from each other if we will only take the time to do so. At the time I was hired, I was immediately faced with having to hire five teachers within three weeks. How frustrating it was to tackle this very important task at the end of the summer! A willing team of teachers and our new secretary took it upon themselves to not only aid me in my duties, but also to play the role of recruiter. Before long we were all ready to start a new year and had added many new staff members who proved to be wonderful teachers.

The entire school staff constantly worked together to teach and model for children what it truly means to learn, grow, and live in our faith. The students taught me that I am seen as an example. My words and actions must continually strive to reflect Christ. As the eighth-grade class was preparing for confirmation, I had three girls ask me if I would be their confirmation sponsor. When I asked one of them why she chose me for this honor, she responded "Because I want to strive to treat others as you do, with love and joy." These words have often been a source of inspiration during times when I have doubted my impact on the lives of children.

The Men's Club taught me to believe in my dreams and reach for the moon. This group was always wanting to know what they could do for the school, how they could help out. It was these men who were responsible for remodeling an entire house in order to open a Pre-K program and reviving the "hot lunch" program. No matter what our needs are, they always strived to make the school a better place for our children.

My experience with the board of education gave me the ability to find value in the views of others. Although parts of the community did not always see eye to eye on an issue, the board made it a priority to hear all sides. While the board members challenged the views of one another, they also found a way to compromise for the good of Saint Patrick.

Catholic education is a culture. Parents who have experienced Catholic schools are likely to send their children to Catholic schools. In the community of St. Patrick this was truly the case. The parents, grandparents, and alumni of the school were involved in every aspect of the school. Their desire and commitment to making St. Patrick a wonderful school for future generations was evident in all they did. They drove their children from other parts of the city to attend St. Patrick, volunteered their time, and did what they could to support the school. These people were a constant reminder that we were all there for the children, and wanted them to have the best opportunities possible.

I have heard numerous times that being a principal is a lonely job. However, I have found that is not always the case. You must learn to rely on those around you for support and encouragement. Sometimes those you come to rely upon are not just in your parish, but outside of it as well. My pastor, Father Paul Worm, guided me and supported me through the rough days and the easy days. His trust in my abilities gave me strength during the strongest storms. The superintendent, Dr. Mike Rockers, taught me how to truly listen to others, not only with my ears, but also with my heart and with my actions. The principals in the area were wonderful listeners as well as mentors to someone with so many questions. Last but not least was Sister Lucille. As a Sister of Mercy she had served as principal of St. Patrick for over 20 years. Her wisdom, her smile, her guidance and her prayers were the strongest support I felt that year. Sometimes we just have to look around us for the professional support network that exists.

During my first year as principal, I learned what a community is capable of. A community is a group of people brought together for a common goal. For St. Patrick, and all Catholic schools, that goal is to spread the Good News, to educate and raise our children with a strong and willing faith. The school community does not only consist of those who are in the building on a daily basis; it also consists of those around it who support and pray for the school. Those whose lives have been touched by a teacher, a student, or a member of the community sharing in God's love are also part of the school community.

My parents had always told me that the Lord would never give you more than you could handle. As an adult I started to believe their words, but never as much as I did my first year as principal. The difference people can make in the lives of others never ceases to amaze me. We may never know the impact of our actions on others. I just pray that I have made the difference in the life of a child in the way the St. Patrick community made a difference in my life. As a first-year administrator, I was fortunate to learn what it meant to be a part of a community that treasured its Catholic faith.

Jesus and Joy for the Journey

Kathleen A. Barton
Santa Maria del Popolo
Mundelein, Illinois

My first year as a principal was exciting, rewarding and somewhat intimidating all at the same time. After over 15 years in the classroom and countless hours of study to earn my Master's Degree in Administration, I thought I knew what I was in for. However, as most first-year principals will confess...nothing truly prepares you for the reality of the day-to-day responsibility of educating hundreds of students mainly through the efforts of several dozen adult staff.

Although being a new principal is difficult at times, it is always very rewarding. This is especially true when nearly everything is new. One of the joys of the position is getting to pick a theme for the school year. I chose "Jesus and Joy for the Journey."

There were several reasons that I chose that theme. I certainly felt that my efforts to become a principal had indeed been a personal journey. A popular saying goes something like, "success in life is not a destination, it is a journey." Well, you can modify that to say that being a principal is not a destination, it too is a journey.

While not always easy, the first year was truly a joyful time for me, in the sense of being able to learn new things and growing with confidence in my ability to do the job. I also felt the presence of Jesus all along the way.

During the time of preparation, my prayer had been that the Lord would guide me to a school where my talents and abilities would be most needed. I was lucky to find such a place at Santa Maria del Popolo. This is a loving community filled with enthusiastic people who believe strongly in the value of a Catholic education. Parents and teachers alike seemed to want the best for the students. The school's mission statement expresses a desire to "provide a Catholic education of excellence." I felt that from the very beginning this was a good place for me to begin my journey as a Catholic school principal.

Not long after I first arrived, I met a group of parents who shared my vision to enhance the Catholic identity symbols within the school and in general to beautify the facility. We formed the Beautification Committee. The group studied what needed to be done and developed a work plan.

One of the ideas in the work plan was a wall mural of Jesus and the children. To be positioned at the entrance to the school, the mural would show our children dressed in their uniforms standing with Jesus. One of our mothers drew the picture and painted it on the wall with a welcome sign above. There would be no doubt as to the Catholic presence in our school now.

The next project involved a parish hall. Our school does not have a gymnasium, and so all the activities take place in the parish hall. This space had not been renovated in many years and was not an inviting place. Our wonderful Beautification Committee rolled up its sleeves and began the work of painting the walls and ceiling, replacing the floor, and wrapping the posts with new mats (a safety precaution).

Other parents were eager to be a part of the renovations and contributed their time and talents. In addition, we received almost $25,000 in donations. One student's parents who owned the local hardware store gave us a charge account at their store to buy the necessary materials and paint. They never sent us a bill. I was also able to purchase new lunchroom tables and chairs with some of the money because we also use the hall for our cafeteria.

Another parent who owned a tile store donated an entire floor for the parish hall as well as several smaller rooms that are connected to the hall. He also provided the crew to install the tile at a greatly reduced cost. Other parents painted the school name and spirit symbol on the walls. It was truly an all-school effort.

The generosity of these parents and friends of our school overwhelmed me. Most of all the parishioners were pleased with the school's efforts and were grateful to us for beautifying the space that we all share.

The entire project involving the Beautification Committee and the spirit of giving from so many people with its benefits to the school, and most importantly, the students, was definitely my most rewarding experience during my first year as a principal. The Spirit was at work in our school and it showed.

I learned that often there is a strong desire by the parents and the community to help and improve their school. The principal can be the catalyst to get things started by organizing the effort and helping to identify what needs to be done. Then the principal should step back and let the volunteers roll up their sleeves. The results can be fantastic.

New Effort Brings out Forgotten Beauty

Catherine Moore
Our Lady of Lourdes Catholic School
Salt Lake City, Utah

I was named principal of Our Lady of Lourdes Catholic School in the spring of 1999. The school facility was built in 1964 in order to serve "children of God" in developing faith and knowledge. While the mission to provide an excellent education has been maintained for the past thirty-six years, the upkeep of the building has slowly deteriorated.

On my first official tour of the school, I was aware of the cluttered, dark and dingy hallways. The unkempt appearance did not speak of a child-centered learning environment for the students. On succeeding visits, I became more and more concerned about the physical condition of my new educational home. Providing clean classrooms, restrooms and common areas quickly became the priority for the summer month's work. Setting the goal that the students would begin the school year in a clean and safe environment was the single most important decision that I made in the early days of my administration.

My first actions were to go through storage areas and clear out hallways. Our dumpster was filled numerous times with collections of out-dated books, dusty boxes of recycled papers and a variety of broken machines and computers. There was even a large stash of used fluorescent lights. As one entered the school, the space was cramped with an unsightly metal locker/coat rack, rolls of bulletin board paper, fake decorative trees and two life-size statues of Our Lady of Lourdes and St. Bernadette. The clutter found new places in the now empty storage areas or the city dump. The statues were moved outside and set in a natural garden in front of the school. Feelings of openness and warmth greet all that enter our building. Our hope is that the physical welcome is matched with personal warmth and concern.

Now that it was possible to walk through the hallways, I realized underneath several years of wax and dirt build-up there was a beautiful terrazzo floor. A professional cleaning company was hired to strip and clean the floors. Two men would work all night; and any help that could be found would move desks in and out of classrooms during the day. I would arrive at the school about 7:30 a.m. to find the cleaners waiting to show off the dazzling floors that were a result of their night's work. Each morning a larger contingent of staff and admirers gathered to "ooh" and "aah" over the transformation. Within a week, the school took on a whole new appearance. As teachers started to decorate rooms and plan for the opening days of school, a sense of pride energized their preparations.

The greatest challenge of all was dealing with the restrooms. One of the students told me, "The bathrooms are disgusting." Not only were they disgusting, but they were also down right ugly - victims of a mixture of left over paints. With lots of elbow grease, the restrooms were cleaned. A parent painted the walls and stalls in colors coordinated with the tile. Another family made the commitment to clean the restrooms every day during the school year.

As the doors opened for the first day of school, there was a collective sigh of wonder over the shining cleanliness greeting parents and students. The positive support that I have received from parents and faculty began with their initial pleasure of seeing the school as a clean center for learning. They continue to comment on the transformation that has occurred. Now a steady stream of students come to my office to complain about other students who do not share in the responsibility for picking up papers or leaving the bathrooms in order. Students take pride in trying to keep the school clean. Student Council leaders organize clean-up days in which each class is assigned an area to improve.

Our work is not completed. An extensive list of needs has been prioritized according to cosmetic and structural improvements. Each time I enter the second-grade classroom, I am determined to do something about the stained ceiling tiles caused by a roof leak several years ago. Missing ceiling tiles in the seventh grade need to be replaced. A retired gentleman from the parish is refinishing office cabinets. Grant requests have been submitted asking for monies to replace broken entrance doors that can no longer be repaired. Some parents are looking forward to painting classrooms during the summer months. Others are offering ideas and skills for other projects. They are empowered with the desire to make our facility the best possible school for their children.

Painting Old Walls Creates New Sense of Community

Gayle Reider
St. Aloysius School
KauKauna, Wisconsin

When asked to sit down and reflect on my first year as principal and to write about my most rewarding experience, I really had to sit back for a moment and reflect. There were many rewarding experiences.

The one that comes to mind first is the realization that I really have the opportunity to make this the best learning experience for a child that I can. My first goal was to create a warm, welcoming learning environment. I wanted to do something to brighten up our school. The walls were painted a dingy brown.

During the summer a group of parents and teachers painted the hallways and entrances in the entire school. We chose a brighter and lighter color and decorated the lower level of our school with rainbow stripes running down the hall, where Grades 1 – 5 are housed. Parents sewed banners for each Grade to hang by their door. On the school's second level, where our three- and four-year-old preschool students are housed, we painted the hallway white and each door was decorated with age appropriate pictures. This project brightened our school, as the walls had not been painted for 20 years. This spruce-up has made our school a warm and welcoming home for our students. Little changes in environment can have quite an impact on learning.

When the children arrived in the fall we set up a Student Council. A fifth grade president was elected along with a fourth grade secretary. The entire student body voted. Children running for office gave speeches, hung posters and campaigned for votes. Now, each grade sends a representative to our meetings, which we try to hold monthly over lunch.

The Student Council reaches out to those in our communities who have special needs. Some of the projects taken on by the Student Council include: donations to local charities, clothing drives for an abuse shelter, cleaning up school grounds and planting trees on school property, and raising money for a local family whose daughter is suffering from cancer. The Student Council also plans many activities for fun in our school, including our Fall Carnival.

My goal was to make our school a warm and welcoming place. I want people to walk through our doors and feel like they are in the presence of Christ. My intent is that the children see and experience the lesson of reaching out to others as Jesus did. Through community outreach programs they get to experience the good feeling you get when you reach out to others in need.

A final rewarding experience I would like to share is the building of community among the entire faculty, staff, parish and maintenance staff. Each week we gather for prayer and sharing. At this time people are given an opportunity to share ideas and throw out any problems they may be experiencing. We brainstorm and try to come up with a solution or various solutions to help solve the problem.

We also do monthly luncheons. Each teacher or staff person signs up for a month and a team puts on the lunch. The entire staff: janitors, secretaries, parish staff, and faculty are invited. A small fee of $2.00 - $3.00 is charged to cover the cost of the food. We eat together and usually have small prizes at the end.

I have found this activity builds our community and fosters good relations among the entire staff. This also improves the entire staff's relationship with one another. I learned that if the staff is happy, the students are happy and the parents are happy.

This helps us to teach and treat others according to the greatest commandment, "Love one another as you love yourself."

A Breath of (Cool) Fresh Air

BJ Rossow
St. Charles Borromeo School
Albuquerque, New Mexico

I accepted the position of principal at St. Charles School on July 3, 1998. Upon my arrival July 4 to take the keys and view the school, I discovered an assortment of challenges; the largest being the fact that the school had no cooling system. Temperatures inside the school average 103 degrees during the months July through September. I was convinced that by working together as a community, we could obtain permission, secure funding, and complete the entire project of air conditioning the school within one year.

I was alone in this opinion, as everyone felt that because the school was 46 years old it was neither practical nor possible to install a modern cooling system. I was faced with the problem of inertia; people would say to me, "We haven't had a cooling system in 46 years, why do we need one now?" Gradually I won over the pastor, the school board, students, teachers, and parents to my way of thinking. We became determined to go through all the wickets to get a "cool school." The entire St. Charles community contributed to the effort.

Monies totaling $200,000 were raised by students, parents, parishioners including the Holy Name Society, school alumni, and through an assortment of grants and loans. Work commenced the day after school was released for the summer, and on the first day of the new school year our students experienced, for the first time, a comfortable indoor environment.

I am especially proud of this achievement because it showed me the importance of working together with the school community in order to accomplish a common goal.

Chapter 3:
Finding God Everyday on the Job

The Body of Christ

Irene D. Sena
Saints Philip and James School
Phillipsburg, New Jersey

As we experience life from different perspectives, we continue to learn with greater breadth and depth. As the Principal of Sts. Philip and James School, in Phillipsburg, New Jersey, it was my awesome fortune to be blessed by our Pastor, Monsignor Michael J. Corona to become an instantaneous Eucharistic minister. At our fall school mass, Monsignor honored and asked me to assist him in the distribution of communion. Many times I had witnessed and participated in this miracle but never had my hands been an actual instrument of this sharing of the Eucharist with others. It was during those awesome minutes, I realized that this was God's way of giving me practice for my mission as principal. He was relaunching my role as educator with a quantum leap of faith. I comprehended that much of what I would be asked to do as principal would symbolically parallel this experience. As I watched Monsignor Corona changing the bread and wine into the body and blood of Christ, I became aware that I was also changing. For having this experience, I would never be the same. God intensifies specific areas of your life in which He desires you to become most active. He was not only intensifying but indeed, He was giving me a big shove in the direction of choice.

Every day of our lives, we are commissioned to be a Eucharistic Minister, to share Christ's love with others and to distribute CHRIST Himself and all that He embodies. Daily as principal of Sts. Philip and James School, I am beckoned with finding the correct, the best path into each child's, faculty member's, parent's heart and soul. While distributing the Eucharist, those who keep their hands high in anticipation of the reception of the Lord and those who are less obvious as to how they are ready to cradle the host challenged me. The same challenge is mine each day as an administrator: how to serve each person, how to find that right path in which to offer the essence of Christ which is within each person to share. My continual mission is to seek that point of entry and serve.

I felt that the community viewed me from a different perspective. They saw me alongside the pastor distributing Communion and they looked for my strength to lean on and my humility in the gift of giving.

As I stood, carefully placing communion hosts in hands and on tongues, I was aware of my role of holding Christ in my heart for all to see and in my hands for all to receive.

"AMEN"

Prayer and Scripture Get New Message Across to One and All

Mary Margaret Hitt
St. Helen Catholic School
Pearland, Texas

After many years of praying and beseeching the Lord for a principalship, I am indeed blessed with the job I have now as principal of St. Helen Catholic School. Although being educated in both parochial and public schools and receiving my higher education from the Basilians at the University of St. Thomas in Houston, my teaching career prior to my new administrative position has been strictly in the public venue. I cannot express the excitement I had upon being offered the job as principal in a Catholic school. Enthusiasm consumed me at the thought that I could now freely express my deep faith in my Lord and pray with my students and staff, unlike public school where "teacher-led" expressions of faith were strictly prohibited. This ability to express my faith in Jesus, my Savior, including using the scriptures, is my most rewarding experience.

One blessing I have is the ability to pray the scriptures with my staff. We begin faculty meetings and often begin one-on-one conferences with prayer or a scriptural reading.

In addition, we have morning prayer in our teachers' lounge area that includes prayer requests or praise reports. Often we use scripture as a reflection to start our day. Prayer and the Word of God help us to focus on where we want to go and how we wish to get there. It is a blessing to be able to pray prayers of healing, of praise, of reconciliation, and of hope with each of them. The ability to use the Word of God has strengthened me in hard times.

Prayer and the Bible have girded me up during times of trouble, and these have been many for a first-year principal. I have stepped into a leadership position where guidelines and consistency have been lacking. Although only a third-year school, no administrator has ever stayed more than a year due to unforeseen circumstances. Clearly a culture and a climate needed to be created. Because of my consistency in decision-making and enforcement of guidelines and policies, I have met with some unhappy patrons who believed rules were for all except them. Despite student withdrawals, words spoken in anger, scathing letters with copies to the bishops of our diocese, His Good News and prayers have truly been a light on a sometimes dark path. Personally, I have stood firm on the principle from Genesis 50:20 where Jacob's son Joseph, who had been sold into slavery by his brothers, states, "Even though you meant harm to me, God meant it for good, to achieve His present end, the survival of many people." Change is not easy for anyone, but I see positive changes happening here at St. Helen Catholic School. We have many fine families and they and their children are committed to our school. St. Helen Catholic School faculty is among the best I have ever seen. We all use prayer and scripture to lift up the school as a whole and each other's personal needs. In addition to being a tool for solace, prayer and the scriptures allow us to teach as Jesus did.

Prayer and scripture were used by Jesus to get His message across. As part of our quality Catholic education, we use prayer and scripture to proclaim the message of the Gospel. We use prayer and scripture to reach over curriculum lines, and it is even integrated in our discipline management plans.

Students who come into the principal's office receive prayer as part of the reconciliation process. Teachers also utilize prayer as an instrument towards positive behaviors. We want the students of St. Helen Catholic School not only to memorize the Word of God, we want them to plant the scriptural seeds down deep into their hearts and apply its meaning to their lives.

Being a first-year principal is like going to a new job every day because of the variety. Every day is different and exciting. Perhaps in my naiveté, I expected smooth sailing and few, if any, problems. God has given me the strength and the tools to withstand the snares of the enemy and those tools are the prayers of our rich Catholic tradition along with prayers from our hearts confirmed through His Word. Because without fear I can freely speak those words of prayer and scripture aloud and model them for my staff and students, this blessing of the freedom to pray and to use the scriptures is indeed my most memorable experience as a first-year principal.

Christian Values Send out Positive Message

Jean M. Doell
Sacred Heart School
Watertown, New York

When I accepted the position of principal, I knew the biggest thing I had to offer Sacred Heart School was my love for the school. I had been a student here for ten years and had taught here for sixteen years, and there is so much I want to give back in honor of all the wonderful sisters and lay teachers who dedicated their lives to our school community. As my first year as a principal at Sacred Heart School is winding down, I am able to say with enthusiasm, "I love my job!"

During the first seven months of school, the enrollment has increased by 11% or 22 students in grade pre-K to eight. We have worked very hard to get our name out in the community and this effort has played a big part in our increased enrollment.

The strategy behind our marketing effort is to present ourselves as an active and contributing member of our community. Our surrounding area is supportive of our school, and good citizenship and Christian concern require that we give back. The publicity and marketing that result are, in a sense, a fringe benefit.

The local public television station offers us several opportunities during the year to man phone banks for their membership drives and TV auction. A group of faculty and parents wear school tee shirts and hang a school banner as they assist public television and receive free airtime.

Our school community sponsored a platoon from our local U.S. Army base when they were on an overseas assignment. We wrote letters and sent packages as a morale booster during their deployment. Now the troops will visit our school and will participate with us in the Armed Forces Day Parade in our city. It may be another newsworthy event. It will at least make our school better known among the local military community.

On Saint Patrick's Day, our school entered a float in the city's parade. It's fun for the families who participate, we are joining in a community celebration, and our name is paraded down Main Street.

We contact the local television stations in hopes that they will consider some events held at school to be newsworthy. One station came to video our Blessing of the Animals for the feast of St. Francis of Assisi. When our community was involved in raising money for the fire department to purchase a thermal-imaging camera, our students held a fundraiser. The other television stations took video footage and did interviews about the fire department visit and our donation. These were more marketing opportunities and we didn't have to tell the public who we are. The activities we were involved in spoke for that message.

Submitting pictures and articles to our diocesan Catholic newspaper on a regular basis resulted in our All Saints' Day celebration receiving front-page coverage. Our fifth grade makes monthly visits to a local nursing home. Since May is National Nursing Home Month, our students will participate in special activities with the residents. Besides the wonderful benefits to both the young and old, it will be a story our Catholic paper may find of interest.

Because we have a unique program in our school—American sign language is taught to all grades by a hearing-impaired parent—we invited the city newspaper to visit and do a story concerning not only the sign language but also how our students are developing a greater sensitivity for the handicapped. The story was a feature article in the Lifestyles section of the paper.

Sacred Heart School has received a great deal of publicity by simply making it known to the local media what unique and interesting things are happening at our school. As part of our mission, we become involved in service and outreach, and then we tell our story to whomever will listen. With a shoestring marketing budget, we have found great success with this approach. Our increased enrollment attests to the fact that people recognize who we are and what we do.

Catholic Values Joyfully Expressed – at Last

Resurrection Parish School
Rosemary Nowotny
Jacksonville, Florida

The year 1999-2000 has been one of the most exciting years of my life. Not only did my youngest child graduate from college; both my children married fantastic Christian soul mates leaving my husband and me alone again after 27 years. After a 30-year career as a teacher and administrator in public schools, I decided to change the course of my life and apply for a principalship in a Catholic school. I accepted a new assignment as Principal of Resurrection Parish School in Jacksonville, Florida.

The greatest challenge of my job has also been the most rewarding experience of my first year as principal of a Catholic school. For thirty years I have been conditioned to suppress my faith and Catholic values and never, ever mention Jesus' name. How sad! As the spiritual leader of a Catholic school it is my job to promote a living and conscious faith among the students and the staff. My personal vision statement has been my guide: "To find happiness, fulfillment and value in living, I will lead a life centered in Christ."

It is so precious to begin each school day with a prayer of thanksgiving and to ask for God's blessing for the safety and success of our students, and to call upon him to help us or our loved ones in a time of need. I can call upon Jesus when I make difficult decisions during the day. I can ask students "What would Jesus do?" when they are faced with the challenges of life. I can pray out loud or silently with a student, staff member, or parent who is seeking spiritual guidance and strength. I can join my students in songs of praise and glory; and I can celebrate mass with the children who have worked so diligently to prepare the liturgy, choose the music, and practiced presenting the gifts. What a joy to have a job that allows me to love and serve the Lord!

The gifts I receive from my job are numerous: the tight hug around my hips from a PK or Kindergartner, the drawings of hearts and flowers with the words "I love you", the birthday cookies and cupcakes, the exciting news of a student's success, and the sweet kisses that grace my hand, arm or cheeks. Recently during a Parish Clean-Up Day, the windows in our school were washed. Five different parents cleaned my window, each finding a streak that had to be removed. They laughed as they rubbed the spot clean and commented that they wanted me to have a clear vision of our students at play. To me it was a sign of acceptance, gratification, and appreciation. A simple act with a very spiritual meaning.

Spiritually, I need to help our students and staff to continue to be influenced by the values and beliefs of Catholicism. As a new principal, I am challenged to possess strong faith and firm allegiance to the goals of the Catholic Church in my mission to provide religious and academic leadership. It is my hope that I will grow spiritually during this journey and together with slow and deliberate tending, the heart and soul of Resurrection Parish School will remain strong, and our values will be reaffirmed.

Chapter 4:
Meditating on the Vocation of Being Principal

True Significance and Meaning Revealed after the Fact

Rosemary Costello
Holy Cross School
Champaign, Illinois

The subject of this piece of writing is supposed to be my most rewarding experience as a first-year principal. I've had a great deal of difficulty deciding what that might be. There have been many rewarding experiences: the parents who tell me they think I am doing a good job, the teachers who feel supported by me, and the children who seem content and happy.

I originally was looking for something that would just jump out at me and shout "Rewarding!" I soon realized that that wasn't going to happen. Instead, I realized that what is truly rewarding are these little things I mentioned. They seem little initially, but in the great scheme of life, they are monumental.

As principal there won't be more than a handful of experiences that will shout "Rewarding!" Being principal is a lot like any other job; the rewards appear small but really add up to something significant. During my 27 years as a teacher, I know that I would not label each day as "Rewarding." But, looking back over my career, it has been rewarding. So many students over the years have said to me how much they appreciated what I did and how much Holy Cross School means to them. They didn't know it at the time; only later did they realize this.

The same applies to being a principal. It really applies to all of life. Our goal here is not to seek our own immediate happiness, but to seek eternal happiness. The most rewarding experience will take place much later in our life.

I became a principal because I love the children and love helping them become all they can be. Knowing that I am directing and guiding their lives is important to me. This in and of itself is rewarding. Being a spiritual leader as well as an educational and instructional leader has been a challenge to me. It has forced me to examine my own spiritual life and direction. I have become a better person for this. What is important is not necessarily what I have done as principal, but what I have become as principal. I have become closer to God and, therefore, closer to others. I am grateful for this opportunity.

Reflecting on the Past Reveals a Bright Future

Sally Hermsdorfer
St. Augustine School
Memphis, Tennessee

Throughout the five days of the 2000 NCEA Beginning Principals Academy, I was reminded of what I have heard countless people say at the end of countless religious retreats: "I didn't know what to expect, and I tried to get out of going at the last minute, but I'm really glad I came."

I will still continue searching for what several colleagues and I came to refer to as "the manual;" a book that would say, "Okay, in August you do this and in September you do this." "The manual" would also have subchapters entitled, "This is how you hire good teachers," and "This is how you end difficult parent conferences on just the right note," and "These are the sequential steps for board formation and pastoral relations," and "This is what you do about the janitor." To my dismay (or perhaps it was more like finding out there's no Santa Claus – a mixture of dismay and developing acceptance of reality) "the manual" doesn't exist.

I may yet write that manual. However, spending five intense days with new principals from all situations educated me in ways no handbook could. Listening to presentations by some gifted and imaginative educators, and enjoying lots of conversation and commiseration, was a pretty good recipe for renewal and hope.

Conventional wisdom, probably more so in the world of Catholic schools, holds that "principalship" is a code word for "martyr," "sacrificed lamb," or "punching bag." I have heard Catholic schoolteachers say such things all through my career, and have watched principals live out those roles. I don't recall hearing it defined as a call to ministry or a charge to joy; at least, I never had reason to reflect personally that it was.

In the eight months that I have been an administrator I more or less figured that I would meditate on my job as vocation "as soon as things calm down a little." And, of course, things never did. The "getting away" aspect of the Academy, the comfortable surroundings, the opportunity for adventure, the advice from knowledgeable authorities, and the constant affirmation from the NCEA were really an immersion into introspection. I heard things, and wrote things, and said things to table partners that truly had never formed fully in my conscious mind while I was speeding through the day-to-day in my office.

The idea of "embracing the chaos" resonated deeply enough to be felt somewhere around my spinal column. What a reassuring notion, that our role as principal of this busy process called a Catholic school is not warden, predictor, policeman! Some of my colleagues were obviously ahead of the learning curve on that one; but for me and many others I spoke to, this discussion was a true benediction.

We newly-minted principals vented to each other, often saying things we couldn't say back home because somebody there might misinterpret and use our frustration to churn up controversy. Certainly, I came into my office the day after the Academy at 6:30 AM to find that the mail and the phone list and the teachers had five days worth of untold surprises in store for me. The Academy didn't fix that. Nor do I believe for a minute that the retreat has solved my problems, or caught me up professionally to five or ten or twenty year principals. But it has gotten me excited about possibilities. For the first time in eight months I can see myself as a five- or ten- or twenty-year principal.

I have always believed that, "There's everything, if there's hope." It gave me such hope to hear that there were others, confident and educated like me, who acknowledged a little pea of fear that they would not succeed, that they would alienate their teachers or parents or pastors or school boards, or in some other way pave the path for disaster at their schools. It gave me hope to see what greenhorns like myself were already accomplishing, often against incredible odds or in the face of great challenges. It was good to laugh together and to pray together, and I am very, very glad my superintendent refused to let me back out.

Spreading Happiness through Fulfillment of a Dream

Denise E. Mulcahy
St. Patrick's School
Sheldon, Iowa

Ever since I can remember I have wanted to be a principal in a Catholic School. When I think about it, I can almost pinpoint when I decided (and why) being a principal was my dream. It happened when we moved and when we met Sr. Catherine. She was the kind of woman who had a lot of energy and love for what she did. She brought my family in, helped us to adjust and catch up, and she also got to my parents and involved them in the school. After spending time with her and watching her interact with teachers, parents, and students I decided that I would be a principal in a Catholic school someday...and here I am!

This year has been one of many learning experiences. I won't lie – there have been times of tears and frustration as well as laughter and enjoyment, but overall – this has been a good year. There are many things I have done this year that I am proud of and that have been rewarding for me, and it is hard to pick just one. I do believe that a major role of the principal is to encourage and build up teachers and of all the things I have been able to do this year, what I have done in that area is what I have found to be the most rewarding.

All the books you read about teaching say that positive reinforcement, lots of affirmation, and specific praise is what is important in helping kids to learn. The same is true for what principals can do for teachers. By letting them know - and often and honestly - that they are appreciated and are doing a good job helps them learn and improve their teaching abilities. With all this in mind, I set out to make sure that the teachers at St. Patrick's knew this and felt this as often as I could. I think it became so important to me because I came from a school where I knew I was appreciated and I wanted to give that same good feeling to the teachers here.

One of the things that I do is to write thank-you notes throughout the year. Each teacher received a note on September 25 – one month after school started. The note was not lengthy, but I told them that I appreciated their hard work and picked out one specific thing that I had seen them do or heard them say and put that in the note, too. I have tried to give out thank-you notes throughout this entire year. It is rewarding to sit back and watch the teachers read the notes and walk away feeling a little bit better about themselves that day.

So many things happen in a classroom that the teacher may not think are any big deal because they do it all the time – or it is always there (like a bulletin board), but noticing the little things makes a big difference. Our eighth-grade teacher does a sign-language unit with the students. She shares with them about her brother who uses sign language to communicate and then they learn letters, words, and prayers. For her, this unit happens each year, but as a new person I saw a lot of excitement in her and in her students as they worked on this. I had kids coming up to me and showing me how to say the Our Father in sign language. With things like this and other little things (that are really big things), I try to leave post-it notes for the teachers congratulating them on what they have done. It makes me feel good when they read it and smile to themselves. It doesn't take very long – but the effect lasts a really long time! And I like to think that when I do something like this for the teachers, they will do these same kinds of things for the students.

Along with the positive notes and comments for the teachers I have tried hard to make sure that all of the staff feel good about themselves. From the secretary, to the janitor, to the cooks, I try to visit them often and to leave them thank-you notes as well. They tell me how nice it is to be a part of the school and not just the one who cleans the school or prepares the meals, and that makes me feel good too.

Obviously I am a letter writer and note writer, but I don't save this only for the teachers, I write notes for the students as well. Our primary grades receive progress reports about once a month. Each time I look through the reports, I jot a quick note to each child about their progress. I keep notes in a notebook about each one and then I can relate what I read this time with what I read from before. The kids love the notes and their parents have commented on how much they appreciate the time I take to do that. I know the kids like it because they tell me they have their notes all over the refrigerator or bulletin boards at home. It does not take very long, but it is worth every minute.

Being a principal is the fulfillment of a dream that I have had since I was in grade school. I believe that being a principal in a Catholic school should involve more than just day-to-day running of the school, worrying about the budget, and writing the newsletter. By virtue of the fact we are about life with God, I believe it is my job to try to bring people close to Him by my words and actions. There have been days, I can honestly say, that I thought I would not make it. But I do. I come back here the next day, and I realize that I can do anything because I have faith in myself and faith that the many prayers I say each day do not go unheard. This is what makes this job rewarding. This is what makes me glad that all those years ago I decided to become a principal in a Catholic school.

Support from all Sides in a New Calling

Kathryn Lawrence
St. Martin of Tours
Cincinnati, Ohio

Support was my most rewarding experience as a new principal. The support came in many different ways. The first outward sign of support was from my staff at our opening faculty meeting before school started. I was very nervous that day. It was the first time that I worked with my staff as a whole. This meeting was my first test of really showing good leadership. It would set the tone for the year. Our meeting opened with a prayer service specially crafted to follow our theme for the year. First on the agenda was in-servicing my teachers on the new regulations regarding Professional Development. The archdiocese was implementing the first year of Individual Professional Development Plan and it was my job to present the plan to the faculty so that they could understand the process. This was followed by all the nitty-gritty business that needs to be done to start school - Supervision schedules for yard duty, detention duty, etc. When the meeting was completed, my faculty gave me a round of applause. It was not that I did such a terrific job with that first meeting, but as a genuine show of support that they would cooperate with me. I came home from that meeting feeling empowered - I could do this job.

Another valuable source of support was from my former principal and two other teachers who became principals from the school from which I came. My former principal called me up, plus the other two, and asked if we wanted to go out for dinner. By this time we were eager to get together to share our experiences. This one dinner led to monthly dinners. Each month we gathered to share what was going on in our schools, what problems we were having, and a chance to ask any question to which we needed a solution. The regular principal meetings often did not lend themselves to this type of informal exchange. It was at these meetings that I again felt reinforcement; I could do this job.

A more formal means of support were the meetings that the Archdiocese had for new principals. These meetings kept us up-to-date and gave us more individualized help on current tasks that needed to be done. In this way we did not become lost in the bigger crowd of principals at the diocesan meetings. At the final meeting of the year we were to bring a symbol of our first year of principalship to use in our closing prayer service. I brought with me a book of matches. Everyone laughed when I explained my symbol. The book of matches represented my first year as a baptism of fire. My first year as a principal dealt with the construction of a new parish center, a long term illness of a teacher fighting cancer, she gave me this news on the fourth day of the school year, and in midyear dealing with a pregnancy of one of our students. These are the things for which no college course can prepare you.

This is why I say that the three means of support I received the first year were my most rewarding experience as a first-year principal. It was what helped me through the year. I suggest that every new principal find a support group of three or four principals with whom to relax and share concerns.

In addition to these means of support, the most rewarding experiences were the interactions with the students. The positive reinforcement they give comes in many ways. For example, they performed a great Christmas concert, they generously raised $3000 in pennies for the missions, and the primary students are always ready with a hug. These are what made the first year rewarding.

Chapter 5:
Student Love and Appreciation

A Triumph for Principal and Student Alike

Ruth Mazzarella
Holy Family School
Carteret, New Jersey

Early in October, the fourth-grade teacher asked me to speak to one of her students about her grades. The child was failing miserably and did not seem to be responding to the teacher's warnings. I agreed to speak to the young lady immediately. When the child showed up at my door, I invited her in and motioned for her to sit in the comfortable rocking chair. (Since then, the children have named it the "worry" chair. They tell me it is very soothing to sit and rock when you are sent to the "Principal's office.")

I pulled my chair over to Ashley and began to talk to her about being a fourth grader. She related to me that everything was "Goooood." Each time I asked her how things were going, she responded, "GOOOD." I remember thinking to myself, "How do I tell her things are not so good!" Her teacher had given me her last English test, which was a 44% out of 100%. Gently, I told Ashley that maybe things were not as good as she thought, but that I believed they could get better. I assured her that there was a good English grade inside her, just waiting for her to help it get out. We talked about how she could help good grades get out. Together we planned a course of action. We formulated a "study plan." I told her that I would be very proud of her if she could bring the failing grade to a passing grade by the next chapter test. She left my office smiling and confident that she could improve.

That afternoon, the teacher asked me, "What did you say to Ashley?" The teacher complained that she returned to the room smiling and happy as a lark. When I told her about my conversation with Ashley, she replied very bluntly, "Sending a student to the principal's office will not have much of an effect if they come back looking like they went to the circus!" I replied that I believed we would never get students to perform well by putting them down.

A week or so later, the fourth grade teacher stood at my door with Ashley in tow..."Mrs. Mazzarella, Ashley was something she would like to show you," she announced. I help my breath and whispered a silent prayer; "Dear Lord...please let it be GOOOD!" Ashley stepped forward and proudly presented her latest English test which was much better than passing - it was an "A"! As I bent down to give her a hug, I set my gaze on her teacher. As our eyes met, I recognized an admission of "Maybe you're onto something."

Student Faith Shines in Appreciation

Elizabeth G. Lopez
Santa Clara of Assisi Catholic Academy
Dallas, Texas

As I reflect on the first six months of my principalship at Santa Clara of Assisi Catholic Academy, a number of rewarding experiences come to mind. However, the one experience that seems to stand out above all the others took place on November 17, 1999. This experience really made me aware that one of my primary goals for the 1999-2000 school year was actually being realized.

For the couple of weeks preceding November 17, I was aware something unusual was taking place at school. Walking the hallways I observed the students busily engaged in activities as usual. As I entered various classrooms I noticed papers quickly disappear, or heard the students say to the teacher, "She's coming", and with that came a scurry of little feet towards the closet. Kindergarten announced they had a surprise for me. Pre-Kindergarten were a little less subtle, they simply said, "We're working on a surprise for you, Mrs. Lopez, for Principal's Day." You can always count on the little ones to tell it as it is.

Finally, Principal's Day arrived. Bright and early that morning some upper school students came to my office, with very serious faces, and informed me I was urgently needed in the cafeteria. I left everything and followed them. As I entered the cafeteria all the students stood up and yelled "Happy Principal's Day, Mrs. Lopez." I was then hurried towards a chair at the front of the room and told to sit down. I did so obediently. One by one, small groups of students from each grade came up to me. All held beautifully designed posters with verses from Holy Scripture written on them. The students read each one aloud, and explained why they had chosen that particular verse. One of my favorites was: *Anyone who hears my words and puts them into practice is like the wise man who built his house on rock,* Matthew 7: 24.

The students explained that this verse reminded them of their principal because she always stressed the importance of being Christ-like in words and actions, and that the principal treated each of them with respect, even if they did something wrong.

After each grade had read their verse from Holy Scripture, and beautifully articulated why they had chosen it, my assistant principal came forward. She explained why the school had chosen to focus on the Spiritual dimension of the principal's role, rather than following the general diocesan theme, "Hats off to Principals." Her explanation really touched my heart. She explained that from the very first day I assumed the principal position I had stressed that the number one mission of our school was faith formation. For the first time, she said, the spiritual mission of the school was being placed in its rightful place; it was now the number one priority of the school. She went on to say that Santa Clara of Assisi Academy was now living out its mission, which states, "As an instrument of the church in her capacity as teacher of truth, Santa Clara acknowledges as fundamental the instruction of children in the Catholic faith and their development through formation of conscience are a primary obligation."

Santa Clara of Assisi Catholic Academy was founded in 1994. I am proud to say I was a part of the first faculty of this school. I was also one of the authors of our mission statement. However, as we were a new school we faced all the challenges any new organization faces, including a high turnover in principals and faculty every year. The true mission of the school often became lost in our efforts to just deal with the day-to-day challenges.

I cannot express how much the words of the students, faculty and my assistant principal meant to me. As a Catholic teacher, and now, the principal of a school in which I had worked for four years, I had always believed that faith formation as stated in our mission statement was our number one priority. However, for the most part I had witnessed faith formation pushed to third place, behind academics and athletics. So on becoming the principal I vowed to work towards living up to our mission.

Principal's Day gave me a great boost. The students and teachers reaffirmed that I had articulated the importance of following the true mission of Santa Clara of Assisi Catholic Academy. It made me very aware that my students and faculty had heard my message and were answering the call to follow our mission.

As the first year of my principalship comes to a close I look with fond memories on the year that has passed so quickly, and think back on how very rewarding it truly has been. I hope and pray the years to come will be equally rewarding.